BIG
and
Little

Mary Walker

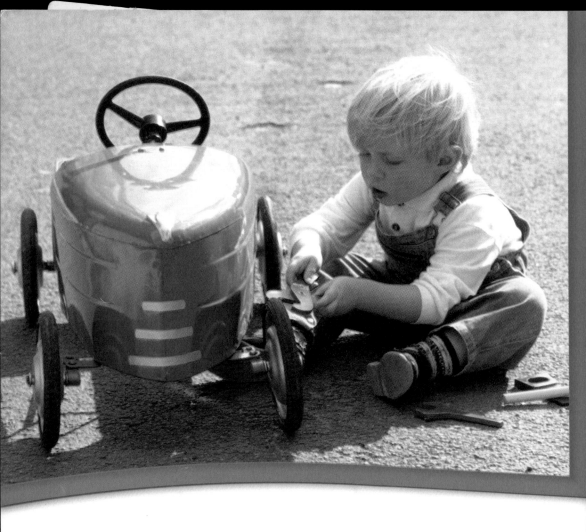

I have a little car.

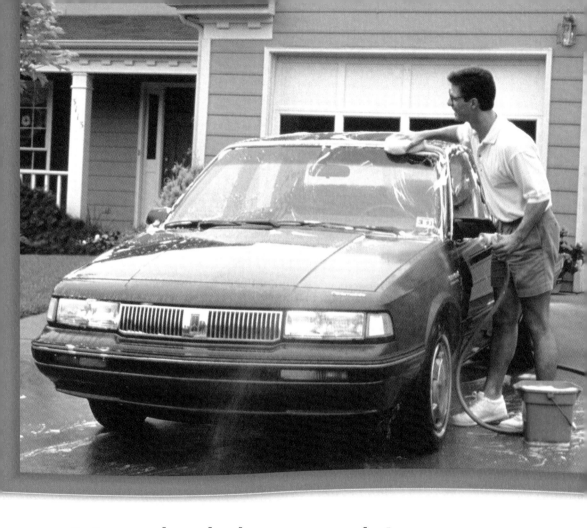

My dad has a big car.

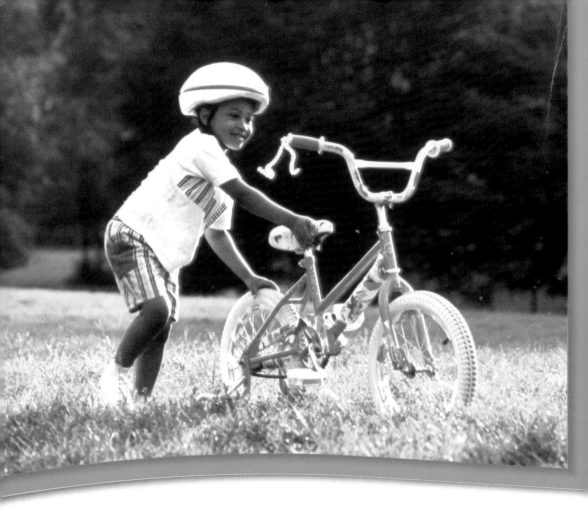

I have a little bike.

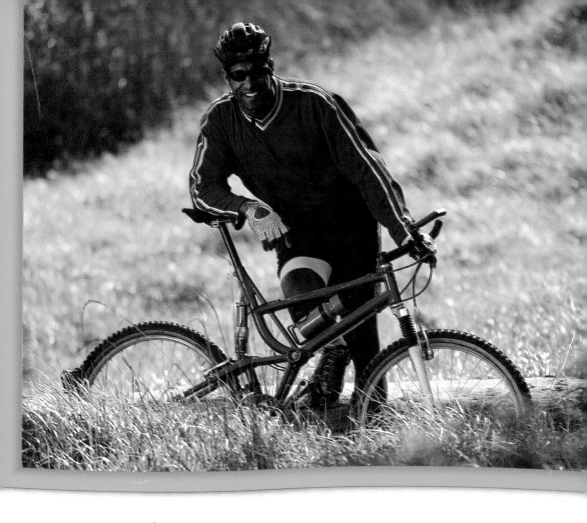

My dad has a big bike.

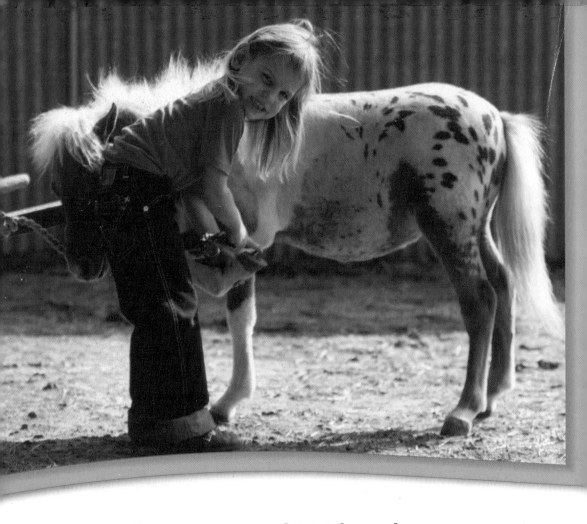

I have a little horse.

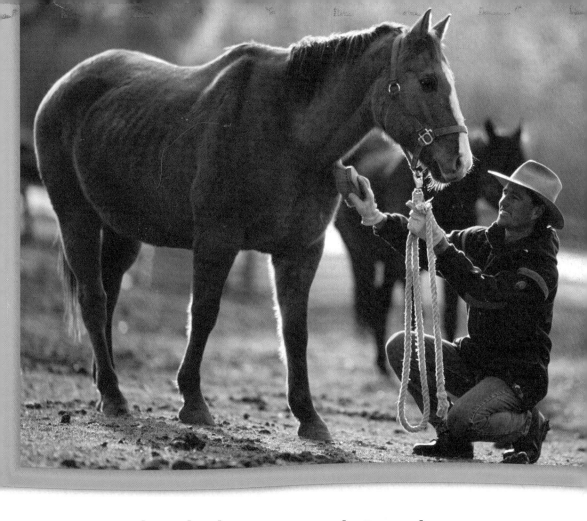

My dad has a big horse.

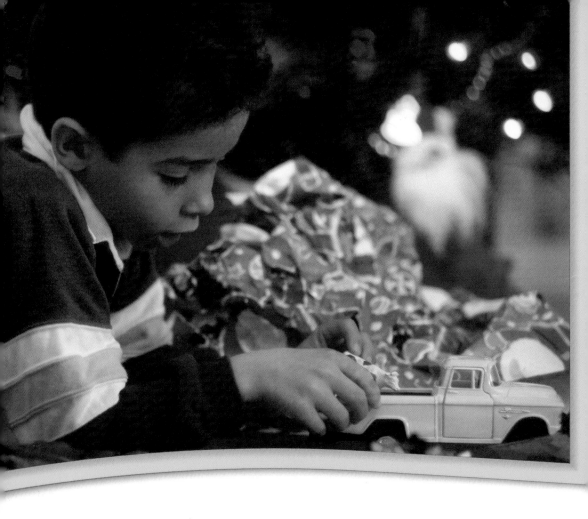

I have a little lorry.

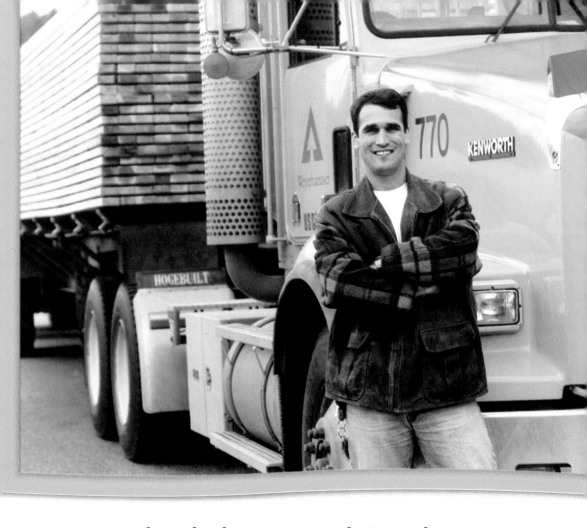

My dad has a big lorry.

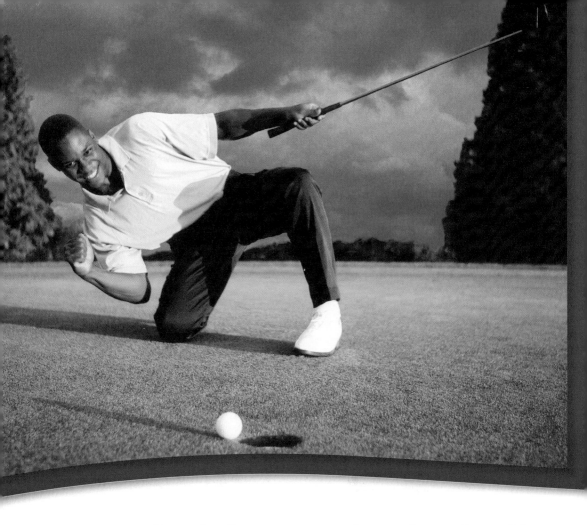

My dad has a little ball.

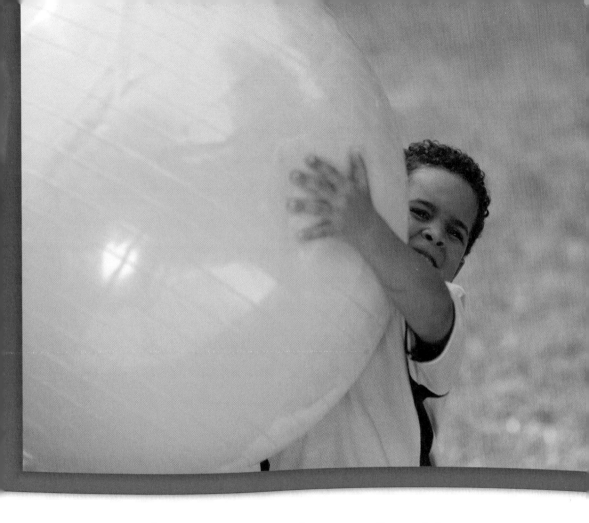

I have a big ball!

Index

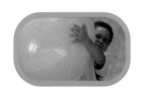
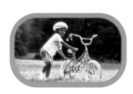
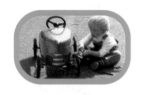
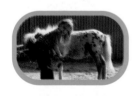
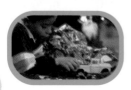